If there is no resurrection of the dead ...

What then?

An exposition of 1 Corinthians 15

By Charles Ozann

ISBN: 978-1-78364-470-4

www.obt.org.uk

****

The Open Bible Trust
Fordland Mount, Upper Basildon,
Reading, RG8 8LU, UK.

If there is no resurrection of the dead ...
What then?

(An exposition of 1 Corinthians 15)

Contents

If there is no resurrection of the dead ... What then? 4

Introduction

If there is no resurrection of the dead ... What then? 6

Introduction

What would you say is the most distinctive, attractive, and far-reaching of all the things we believe? For me the answer has to be **the resurrection.** Though not exclusively Christian since both Judaism and Islam have a doctrine of resurrection of their own, it is nevertheless the most *distinctive* of all our beliefs, and certainly the founder of no other religion claims to have risen from the dead. It is the most *attractive* because it holds out the promise of eternal life on the other side of the grave. And the most *far-reaching* because the resurrection life goes on for ever and ever!

That is why 1 Corinthians 15 is such an important chapter. This chapter tackles the whole subject of resurrection against the backdrop of some who denied or doubted there was any such thing. To the Greek way of thinking bodily resurrection was a ludicrous idea, and there were Jews also, the Sadducees in particular (Acts 23:8), who entertained the same scepticism with less excuse.

If there is no resurrection of the dead ... What then? 7

When Paul spoke of the resurrection of the dead at Athens he was mocked by his philosophical audience and his address was cut short (Acts 17:32). The Greek philosophers were all agreed that death sets one free from the shackles of bodily existence. The immortality of the soul, of the soul alone, was the one thing they looked for.

But for Paul, as for the Bible as a whole, there is no immortality of the soul as if the soul was a spiritual entity that was imprisoned in the body, as thought by Greek philosophers. The soul is the person himself, and our biblical hope is the resurrection of the entire person, body, soul and spirit, not just the body.

Some of the Christians at Corinth were still deeply influenced by Greek philosophy. Their negative thinking on the subject of resurrection was undermining their teaching on salvation and that Christ died for sins and was raised for our justification (1 Corinthians 15:3-4; Romans 4:25). The whole church was in danger of going off the rails if this false teaching was not nipped in the bud. This is what Paul sets out to do in the chapter before us.

But what of today? Isn't all this rather academic in the twenty-first century? Far from it! Ask the average believer what he is expecting and hoping for and he will probably say, to go to heaven when he dies and to meet up with family and friends! Like the ancient Greeks he is still committed to the immortality of the soul. He may pay lip service to "the resurrection of the body" in the words of the (so-called) Apostles' Creed, but this is not the main focus of his belief.

Paul never uses the expression "resurrection of the body"; for him it is always the resurrection *of the dead* (see verses 12,13,21,42 and five other places in the New Testament). It is the entire person who dies and the entire person who rises from the dead.

There is no intermediate state mentioned in Scripture. Paul never entertains for a moment the possibility of life after death without the prior resurrection of the dead person. He doesn't even pause to refute the idea. If we aspire to be scriptural in our thinking, we shall want to pay careful attention to what Paul says in this chapter and be firmly committed to the Christian doctrine of "the resurrection of the dead".

The OBT has already published one book on 1 Corinthians 15, namely *The Resurrection Chapter[1]* by Fred Heyman (1997). In the present booklet I shall try to delve a bit deeper into Paul's thinking and to confront some of the issues raised by modern scholars. I would like to express my gratitude to Brian Sherring and Roger Barnett for their constructive criticisms.

---

[1] See pages 69 and 70 for details of this book.

1 Corinthians
Chapter 15

If there is no resurrection of the dead ... What then?   12

1 Corinthians 15

15:1-2: *Now I would remind you, brothers, of the gospel I preached to you, which you received, in which you stand, and by which you are being saved, if you hold fast to the word I preached to you – unless you believed in vain.*

The first word, *gnorizo*, means "I make known", but is usually translated "I remind" because the Corinthians had already heard and received the gospel as the verse goes on to say. But Paul now finds it necessary not only to remind them, but to make it known all over again because some of them at least had failed to take it on board. Similar is Galatians 1:11,

> "For *I would have you know*, brothers, that the gospel that was preached by me is not man's gospel …"

The Galatians were questioning the divine origin of Paul's gospel just as the Corinthians were questioning the content of it. In both cases Paul had to re-state the truth from first principles while

If there is no resurrection of the dead ... What then?   13

there was still time.

In the case of the Corinthians there were some who were saying "there is no resurrection of the dead" (v.12). This cut at the very core of the Christian gospel because it implied that Christ Himself had not risen from the dead. As Paul says later on (vs.17-19),

> "If Christ has not been raised, your faith is futile and you are still in your sins. Then also those who have fallen asleep in Christ have perished. If in this life only we have hoped in Christ, we are of all people most to be pitied."

That is how important it is to remain firm on the subject of resurrection.

This gospel they had received; they had stood by it and were being saved by it. But unless they held fast to it the whole exercise was in vain. Some of the Corinthians were letting go and drifting back into the pagan error of the immortality of the soul. This drift had to be stopped. Paul felt the same toward the Galatians: "You observe days and months and seasons and years! I am afraid I may have laboured over you in vain" (4:10,11). This is because they had turned back to the weak and worthless principles of the world, putting themselves under the bondage of the Law instead of living by faith, so nullifying the gospel of grace.

15:3-5: *For I delivered to you as of first importance what I also received: that Christ died for our sins in accordance with the Scriptures, that he was buried, that he was raised on the third day in accordance with the Scriptures, and that he appeared to Cephas, then to the Twelve.*

The apostle goes back to the historic facts of first importance, those relating to the death and resurrection of Christ. He does so by means of four clauses beginning with *hoti*, 'that'.

It is the resurrection in which he is primarily interested, but the events stand or fall together.

- If Christ did not rise from the dead, there is no proof that He died for our sins.

- If He was not buried there is no proof that He died at all.

Died and buried are both in the aorist tense indicating an event in the past, but raised is in the perfect tense. That is because the resurrection is more than an historical event: Christ was both raised and remains alive ever since, as the perfect tense denotes. C.K. Barrett puts it well:

> "Christ died, but he is not dead; he was buried, but he is not in the grave; he was raised, and he is alive now."

Against the first and the third (died for our sins and raised on the third day) the apostle adds "according to the Scriptures." There are many Old Testament scriptures which speak of the death and resurrection of Christ, e.g. Isaiah 53; Psalm 22; Psalm 16:10, and perhaps more than we think that point to the third day, e.g. Genesis 22:4; Jonah 1:17; Hosea 6:2.

The apostle now moves on to the five most important appearances of the risen Christ, beginning with Cephas and the Twelve. He mentions only those witnesses who offered the most convincing proof that Christ had indeed risen.

The appearances to the women on the resurrection morning are passed over in silence because the testimony of women might not be accepted. Likewise His appearance to the couple travelling to Emmaus. Instead he concentrates on the most reliable witnesses, apostles well known and respected in the Christian community, whose testimony could be accepted without question. The appearance to Simon Peter is mentioned in Luke 24:34 and to the Twelve in Luke 24:36 and John 20:19.

15:6-8: *Then he appeared to more than five hundred brothers at one time, most of whom are still alive, though some have fallen asleep. Then he appeared to James, then to all the apostles. Last of all, as to one untimely born, he appeared also to me.*

Next He appeared to more than 500 brothers at the

same time. This *could be* the Galilee appearance which He had promised before His death (Matt. 26:32), and which the angel confirmed after His resurrection (Matt. 28:7). The fulfilment is recorded in Matthew 28:16-20. Matthew only mentions the eleven disciples, but the fact that "some doubted" (v.17) points to a larger gathering. If this was not the occasion, there is no record of this appearing and that is the majority view.

Paul says pointedly "most of them are still alive though some of them have fallen asleep." In other words, "If you are still unconvinced, go to Israel and find some of them. They will confirm that what I am saying is indeed the truth!"

The united witness of several hundred witnesses, the majority being still alive, could not easily be dismissed. In the face of such overwhelming evidence scepticism is a dangerous and deceitful stance. Paul challenges his readers to face up to the facts and to abandon their unbelieving doubts.

People today don't have the same advantage; it all

happened so long ago. But those who have examined the evidence most carefully have usually concluded that the resurrection must have taken place just as the Gospels relate. There are some indeed who have set out to prove that the resurrection is a childish fantasy but after studying the evidence have changed their minds. A case in point is Frank Morison, author of the well-known book *Who Moved the Stone?* It was his aim at the outset to prove the absurdity of the resurrection story, but the evidence led him irresistibly to the opposite conclusion!

He appeared next to His brother James. Though not mentioned in the Gospels or Acts, it was probably this appearance which brought James over to saving faith. Pror to this he and his brothers had kept their distance in unbelief (John 7:3-5). Then He appeared to "all the apostles" at the time He ascended into heaven. These five appearances are all connected by the conjunctions *eita* or *epeita*, indicating a succession of events at different times.

Last of all He appeared to Paul himself "as to one

untimely born". According to F. Godet,

> "The strange word *ektroma*, abortion, untimely birth, from *titrosko*, pierce, tear, denotes a child born in a violent and premature way."

In his view,

> "Paul was torn, as by a violent operation, from that Judaism to which he was yet clinging with all the fibres of his heart and will."

There are two other more likely ways in which this word may be understood. It could be said that Paul's conversion was untimely, premature, because it happened suddenly without an adequate period of gestation like a premature baby.

Alternatively, one may think of Paul as anticipating the rebirth of Israel. Israel will be converted at the second coming when they look on the One whom they pierced (Zech. 12:10). Their conversion will be sudden, unexpected and miraculous, like that of Paul. Paul, a type of Israel, anticipated that event like someone born out of due time.

Christ's appearance to Paul was belated so far as His other appearances are concerned, but premature if we think of the conversion of Israel. Either way, Paul makes it clear that he also is a witness of the risen Christ, along with Peter and the Twelve, James the Lord's brother and the large number who saw Him in Galilee.

15:9-11: *For I am the least of the apostles, unworthy to be called an apostle, because I persecuted the church of God. But by the grace of God I am what I am, and his grace towards me was not in vain. On the contrary, I worked harder than any of them, though it was not I, but the grace of God that is with me. Whether it was I or they, so we preach and so you believed.*

As elsewhere Paul is anxious to make clear that he also is an apostle. Though from one point of view he was the least of the apostles because he had persecuted the church of God, he had in fact worked harder than all of them and God had prospered his labours. He also had the distinction of being the only one called the Apostle to the Gentiles (Rom. 11:13) and, as he admits himself, he was not a whit behind the greatest apostles (2 Cor. 11:5). His testimony united with theirs; he spoke with the same authority.

15:12-19: *Now if Christ is proclaimed as raised from the dead, how can some of you say that there is no resurrection of the dead? But if there is no resurrection of the dead, then not even Christ has been raised. And if Christ has not been raised, then our preaching is in vain and your faith is in vain. We are even found to be misrepresenting God, because we testified about God that he raised Christ, whom he did not raise if it is true that the dead are not raised. For if the dead are not raised, not even Christ has been raised. And if Christ has not been raised, your faith is futile and you are still in your sins. Then those also who have fallen asleep in Christ have perished. If in this life only we have hoped in Christ, we are of all people most to be pitied.*

Paul without more ado weighs into his opponents with all guns blazing! He points out the terrible consequences of denying the resurrection of the dead, and especially the resurrection of Christ Himself. But at first sight his train of thought is a bit difficult to follow, so I have prepared a brief analysis which hopefully will clarify his argument.

12 What some were saying: there is no resurrection of the dead

13 False premise: "if there is no resurrection of the dead, then Christ has not been raised"

14-15 "If Christ has not been raised": three consequences
- our proclamation is void
- your faith is void
- we are found to be false witnesses

16 False premise: "if dead persons are not raised, then Christ has not been raised"

17-18 "If Christ has not been raised": three consequences
- your faith is futile
- you are still in your sins
- those who have fallen asleep have perished

19 Paul's conclusion: if there is no resurrection of the dead we Christians are of all men the most pitiable.

Deny the resurrection of the dead and the entire Christian faith falls to the ground. Paul mentions six grave consequences which inevitably follow from this false premise, though two of them are virtually the same.

- The first three are more *practical*. Both his own preaching and their believing are null and void. Worse still, he and his fellow preachers are seen to be false witnesses for having proclaimed something as true which was not true at all.
- The second three are more *theological*. Their faith is profitless, they are still unredeemed sinners, and those who have died have perished for ever. What could be worse than that!

How important it is to hold fast to the doctrine of resurrection, both of the dead in general and of Christ in particular. Without His resurrection our entire faith dissolves into nothing and we are found to be the pathetic dupes of an erroneous fantasy!

15:20-22: *But in fact Christ has been raised from the dead, the firstfruits of those who have fallen asleep. For as by a man came death, by a man has come also the resurrection of the dead. For as in Adam all die, so also in Christ shall all be made alive.*

The words "But now" (translated "But in fact") with which verse 20 begins indicate a sharp change from a negative train of thought to a positive one. One thinks of Romans 3:21,

> "*But now* the righteousness of God has been manifested apart from the law",

or Ephesians 2:13,

> "*But now* in Christ Jesus you who once were far off have been brought near by the blood of Christ."

Verse 20 says

> "*But now* Christ has been raised from the dead, the firstfruits of those who have fallen

asleep."

The word *firstfruits* is used in various connections:

- the firstfruits of dough ("if the dough offered as firstfruits is holy, so is the whole lump", Romans 11:16),
- the firstfruits of Achaia (Rom. 16:5; 1 Cor. 16:15), or
- the firstfruits of redeemed mankind (Rev. 14:4).

There is probably an allusion to the firstfruits of the harvest in Leviticus 23:10-11. The firstfruits are the pledge and guarantee that the rest of the harvest will be gathered in. In the passage before us the risen Christ is the firstfruits of those who have fallen asleep. Those who have fallen asleep include everyone who has died, so the resurrection of all men would seem to be assured.

This is confirmed by verse 22,

"For as in Adam all die, so also in Christ

shall all be made alive."

This is often paraphrased to say,

> "As in Adam all men die, so in Christ shall all (believers) be made alive."

It is argued that "in Christ" does not apply to unbelievers, so it must be believers who are meant. This however is offset by the grammatical consideration that the two *all's* should have the same breadth of meaning. Rather similar is Romans 5:18,

> "Therefore, as one trespass led to condemnation for all men, so one act of righteousness leads to justification and life for all men."

The plain sense is that a new life in resurrection is guaranteed to the entire human race. Christ has conquered death for the entire human race and has won for them a new life in resurrection. But this does not mean that all men will automatically be saved. Christ has won a new life for all men, but for those who reject this new life there is no further sacrifice for sins, but rather the fearful expectation of judgment (Hebrews 10:26-27). There is a resurrection to judgment as well as a resurrection to life (John 5:28-29). The type of person who will forfeit this second life is given in Revelation 21:8. See also 1 Corinthians 6:9-10 and Galatians 5:19-21.

15:23-24: *But each in his own order: Christ the firstfruits, then at his coming those who belong to Christ. Then comes the end, when he delivers the kingdom to God the Father after destroying every rule and every authority and power.*

Verse 23 carries on from versed 22 without a break. They even share the same verb which has to be supplied in verse 23:

> "But each (shall be made alive) in his own order."

The word *tagma*, order or rank, was applied originally to a military phalanx, but later to any grouping, military or civilian. For most commentators there are only two ranks here:

(1) Christ Himself,
(2) Those who belong to Him at His coming.

But if, as we have argued, the two *all's* in verse 22 are co-extensive[2], then a third rank is needed to cover all the rest of the dead. We know from Revelation 20:5,12-13 that in fact the rest of the dead do return to life after the thousand years, so it is natural to find the same programme in 1

----

[2] By co-extensive I mean that the two all's in verse 22 are parallel in meaning. Since undeniably it is *all mankind* who die in Adam, it must grammatically be *all mankind* who will come to life in Christ. There is a universalism in resurrection but not necessarily in salvation, since there are some, especially gross sinners (Revelation 21:8), who will forfeit the new life they have "in Christ" and will be sentenced to the second death instead (Revelation 20:11-15). From the second death there is no reprieve, no further resurrection.

Corinthians.

C.K. Barrett admits that "each in his own group" seems to imply more than is stated in the following words. This difficulty he admits would be set aside if a third rank could be found in verse 24:

> "we should then have a list of three groups, raised up at different times."

But he cannot accept this solution.

> "We cannot find the third group in verse 24; the word does not mean this."

Barrett's problem is of his own making. Verse 22 clearly teaches that *all* shall be made alive and this statement is broken down in the succeeding verses. The return to life will take place in three stages, three ranks:

- first Christ Himself,
- then those that are Christ's at His coming, and
- then comes the end when the rest of the dead

will return to life.

It is only the dogmatic refusal to believe in the millennial reign of Christ which leads Barrett and others to reject this interpretation.

The three ranks of the raised are separated by the conjunctions *eita* or *epeita*: the firstfruits Christ, then (*epeita*) those who belong to Him, then (*eita*) the end.

A similar use of these conjunctions separates the resurrection appearances in verses 5-7. He was seen by Cephas, then (*eita*) by the Twelve, then (*epeita*) by more than 500 brothers, then (*epeita*) by James, then (*eita*) by all the apostles.

Another example of the same construction may be seen in Galatians 1-2. Galatians 1:18, then (*epeita*) after three years I went up to Jerusalem, 21 then (*epeita*) I went to regions of Syria and Cilicia, 2:1 then (*epeita*) after 14 years I went up again to Jerusalem.

Godet says,

"The *eita* implies, in the mind of the apostle, a longer or shorter interval between the Advent and what he calls *the end*."

C.K. Barrett says that an interval is possible,

"but it seems unthinkable that Paul, if he believed in such a kingdom should pass it over without a word."

But in fact Paul has a lot to say about the kingdom. In verse 25 he says that Christ must *reign* until He has put all His enemies under His feet, and in verse 24 that He will deliver the *kingdom* to God the Father after destroying every rule, authority and power.

15:25-28: *For he must reign until he has put all his enemies under his feet. The last enemy to be destroyed is death. For God has put all things in subjection under his feet. But when it says, "all things are put in subjection", it is plain that he is excepted who put all things in subjection under him. When all things are subjected to him, then the Son himself will also be subjected to him who* *put all things in subjection under him, that God may be all in all.*

Verse 25 contains references to Psalm 110:1 and Psalm 8:6. The subjection of all things under Christ's feet is promised in Psalm 8, and His enemies in particular in Psalm 110.

In our passage in 1 Corinthians 15, God puts all His enemies under Christ's feet, the last enemy to be destroyed being death. Godet must be right in saying,

> "The complete victory over death announced in this verse can only be found in resurrection which will extend to all the victims of death without exception."

The destruction of Death and Hades is described in Revelation 20:14 following the resurrection of the rest of the dead after the thousand years. Having given up the dead that are in them, there is no power or place remaining for Death and Hades and they are accordingly thrown into the lake of fire.

The last enemy to be destroyed is death. Death has tyrannized mankind ever since the fall of Adam and Eve. It is the great enemy which everyone dreads and does his best to delay. Yet death continues to mow down whole swathes of mankind every day of the year. How glorious the day when death is finally destroyed!

The destruction of death has in one sense already been accomplished. 2 Timothy 1:10 says that Christ Jesus "*abolished* (same word, *katargeo*, as in 15:26) death and brought life and immortality to light through the gospel." Christ abolished death when He rose from the dead and in consequence all men are assured of resurrection.

Christ's resurrection was the firstfruits, the pledge and guarantee of universal resurrection, but not until the end of the thousand year reign will the process be complete. Then will be accomplished what is written,

> "O death, where is your victory? O death, where is your sting?" (v.55).

If there is no resurrection of the dead ... What then? 35

Some people are perplexed by the statement that

> "the Son himself will also be subjected to him who put all things in subjection under him, that God may be all in all."

Will the Son really be subject to the Father, not simply here and now but throughout eternity? Here it is God who is "all in all", but in Colossians 3:11 it is Christ.

In the body of Christ here and now

> "there is not Greek and Jew, circumcised and uncircumcised, barbarian, Scythian, slave, free; but Christ is all, and in all."

Likewise in Ephesians 1:22, God

> "put all things under his feet and gave him as head over all things to the church."

It is however God who does the subjecting, so the same proviso applies here as in 1 Corinthians 15:27:

"it is plain that he is excepted who put all things in subjection under him."

1 Peter 3:22 tells us that Jesus Christ

"has gone into heaven and is at the right hand of God, with angels, authorities and powers having been subjected to him."

He already has this authority by right, but as Hebrews 2:8 explains,

"At present we do not yet see everything in subjection to him."

This also is what 1 Corinthians 15:24-25 says,

"Then comes the end, when he delivers the kingdom to God the Father *after destroying* ("when he shall have destroyed") every rule and every authority and power. For he must reign until he has put all his enemies under his feet."

Only after that will the Son Himself be subject to

the Father.

We need to distinguish between Christ's essential being and His role as ruler and redeemer. In His capacity as Logos He is equal with God and indeed is Himself God (John 1:1-2), but in His capacity as Son He is subject to the Father. There is nothing strange or objectionable about this.

A similar relationship exists between husband and wife. At the deepest level they are essentially equal, but the wife is nevertheless subject to her husband.

In the body of Christ all members are essentially equal in the sight of God, yet some members are given leadership roles and others more subservient roles. The fact that some are subordinate does not affect their equality and oneness as members of the body.

It would seem that Christ will always be subject to the Father in His capacity as Son, but His essential equality and oneness in the triune Godhead will never be compromised.

15:29: *Otherwise, what do people mean by being baptized on behalf of the dead? If the dead are not raised at all, why are people baptized on their behalf.*

The apostle here returns to the theme of verses 12-19 after the digression of 20-28. In verses 16-19 he spelt out the appalling consequences resulting from the premise "if the dead are not raised." In verses 29-32 he points out the foolishness of their practice with respect to baptism and of his own courageous disregard for his own life "if the dead are not raised." Neither his action nor theirs made any sense if there was no resurrection of the dead.

Again, the question beginning with *ti*, what or why, follows a regular pattern. Verse 29 "*What* will they do, the ones being baptized?" 30 "*Why* am I in danger every hour?" 32 "*What* do I gain (from fighting wild beasts at Ephesus)?" None of these activities were at all reasonable if the dead are not raised.

But what were the Corinthians actually doing? Two very different interpretations clamour for our attention and it is difficult to choose between them.

If the received punctuation is followed with virtually all expositors, we are faced with a situation in which some believers were being baptized on behalf of (or even *over*) their deceased brothers who presumably had died before being baptized themselves. This practice is meaningless, says Paul, if there is no resurrection of the dead. Who in their right mind would want to be baptized on behalf of those whose death is without end, with no resurrection in view? Paul does not condemn the practice; by implication he commends it, or at least condones it. Whatever the merits of the practice it was a complete waste of time if the dead are not raised.

The alternative is to re-punctuate the verse to say,

> "What will they do, those being baptized? For the dead, if dead persons are not raised at all. Why indeed are they baptized for them?"

Baptism signifies death and burial in Romans 6:3-4 and Colossians 2:12, not however death on its own but death followed by resurrection. If there is no resurrection, baptism signifies nothing more than death, and those who offer themselves for baptism are baptized with a view to remaining dead people. They are baptized for the dead, nothing more.

E.W. Bullinger translates:

> "What shall they do who are being baptized? (It is) for the dead if the dead rise not at all!"

In other words,

> "It is to remain dead, as corpses, without hope of resurrection."

B.W. Newton translates:

> "Else, what meaning will there be in the act of those who are baptized? They must be baptized on behalf of their own dead bodies, if dead bodies rise not at all. Why are they

baptized for them?"

The question which requires an answer is whether the words "(baptized) for the dead" and "baptized for them" can be construed to mean

> "they are baptized for (on behalf of) dead people, namely themselves."

I have my doubts, I confess. More naturally, baptized for dead people implies baptism on behalf of *others* rather than themselves. Perhaps therefore we should give preference to the traditional interpretation. Grammatically this presents no problem at all, and the practice implied, though unattested, could easily have arisen. The apostle does not object to it since it was done in good heart and offended no principle of the faith.

15:30-34: *Why am I in danger every hour? I protest, brothers, by my pride in you, which I have in Christ Jesus our Lord, I die every day! What do I gain if, humanly speaking, I fought with beasts at Ephesus? If the dead are not* *raised, "Let us eat and drink, for tomorrow we die." Do not be deceived: "Bad company ruins good morals." Wake up from your drunken stupor, as is right, and do not go on sinning. For some have no knowledge of God. I say this to your shame.*

Paul continues in the same vein, citing his own experiences. I am in peril every hour, he says, I die every day. But where is the gain if there is no resurrection?

> "Humanly speaking, I fought with beasts at Ephesus."

Paul was not prone to exaggeration: if he says he fought with beasts at Ephesus, we may be sure that he did. Grosheide gives a string of reasons why this cannot be taken literally.

- No one survived the arena;
- there is no reference to it in Acts;
- Luke could hardly have omitted such a memorable event;
- Paul himself does not mention it in 2

Corinthians 11;

- a Roman citizen could not be condemned to fight in the arena.

But we do not know the circumstances. The beasts may have been set on him by an angry mob rather than a corrupt judiciary. We know that he had a lot of trouble from the mob at Ephesus, stirred up by Demetrius the silversmith (Acts 19).

If it is true that the dead are not raised, there is more sense in the behaviour of fatalists and cynics who were saying, "Let us eat and drink for tomorrow we die" – quoted from Isaiah 22:13 in a situation which called for weeping and mourning rather than revelry. He implies that the negative attitude which was rife at Corinth was due to their keeping bad company, especially with those who had no knowledge of God such as the Epicurean and Stoic philosophers. In the words of the pagan playwright Menander, "Bad company ruins good morals."

He urges them to wake up from their drunken stupor and to stop sinning. Their attitude was essentially sinful, a stubborn unwillingness to give up pagan acquaintances, habits and ideas, and to embrace the Christian way of life.

15:35-38: *But someone will ask, "How are the dead raised? With what kind of body do they come?" You foolish person! What you sow does not come to life unless it dies. And what you sow is not the body that is to be, but a bare seed, perhaps of wheat or of some other grain. But God gives it a body as he has chosen, and to each kind of seed its own body.*

The question in verse 35 is one arising from rationalistic unbelief, the sort of question the Corinthians were asking. To them it was unreasonable to suppose that a dead body could ever rise from the dead. How could anything so putrid and vile ever come to life again? That is the reasoning of unbelief. To the mind of faith the situation is completely different as Paul goes on to explain. To the eye of faith burying a dead person is like planting a seed. It is true the outer husk will fall away and rot, but the kernel will assume a new body as God decides, and will rise from the earth in resurrected life. That is how we should think of burying our loved ones, as planting a seed which one day will return to life.

A seed may remain dormant in the ground for a very long time. Seeds found in the tombs of the Pharaohs have been known to germinate. When God gives the word, the conditions being right, the seed is activated and springs back to life. If this miracle can be performed for seeds found in the tombs of the Pharaohs, how about the Pharaohs themselves? Will they not also come back to life in due course?

God's seed abides in the believer (1 John 3:9). That seed cannot die. It cannot even sin, let alone die. It may remain dormant in the ground for a long time, but one day (at the second coming of Christ, v.23) it will return to life. Even unbelievers will rise from the dead because Christ has won for them a new life as well, though, as we have seen, this new life may be forfeited by those who refuse to believe.

The rationalist would say that someone who has

drowned at sea and his body eaten by sea creatures cannot possibly rise from the dead. But the Bible says,

> "And *the sea* gave up the dead who were in it" (Rev. 20:13).

If *they* will rise from the dead, so will everyone else. What happens to their bodies is of no consequence – "God gives it a body as he has chosen."

The story is told of an atheist woman who gave instructions that a huge mound of concrete should be placed over her grave as proof to the world that her body could never rise from the dead. It was done as she directed: a seemingly impenetrable mountain of concrete was piled over her grave. It so happened, however, that an acorn got lodged in that concrete. That acorn found a crack in its concrete prison and it put down a feeler. At the smell of water that feeler wormed its way down to the earth below. Now there is a huge oak tree growing on that grave and the concrete blocks have been tossed all around as if made of clay.

If there is no resurrection of the dead ... What then? 47

God is not mocked! That oak tree is proof that this woman will rise from the dead whether she likes it or not. Like the rest of her sort, she will rise from the dead in the second (postmillennial) resurrection when she will be judged according to what she has done.

15:39-42a: *For not all flesh is the same, but there is one kind for humans, another for animals, another for birds, and another for fish. There are heavenly bodies and earthly bodies, but the glory of the heavenly is of one kind, and the glory of the earthly is of another. There is one glory of the sun, and another glory of the moon, and another glory of the stars: for star differs from star in glory. So it is with the resurrection of the dead.*

Two questions are asked in verse 35: How are the dead raised and with what kind of body? They are asked by the Corinthian doubters and imply that the resurrection is impossible. Paul answers the first question in verse 36,

"What you sow does not come to life unless

it dies."

The *manner* of resurrection is illustrated by the annual miracle of dying and rebirth known to every agriculturist. One crop dies and falls into the ground (or is sown) and the next year it comes up again. The same pattern is followed in the world of mankind. They die, fall into the ground (or are buried) and come back to life: Christ the firstfruits, then at His coming those who belong to Him.

The second question (With what kind of body do they come?) is answered in verses 37-39. The short answer is given in verse 38,

> "God gives it a body as he has chosen, and to each kind of seed its own body."

The natural world exhibits an infinite variety of bodies: bodies human, animal, bird and fish, bodies terrestrial and bodies celestial. Moreover, each has its own character, beauty or brightness. The sun, moon and stars all differ in brightness. The sun is very different from the moon in glory, but each has its own place of honour in God's universe.

Why does Paul draw attention to this variety in nature? Is it not to illustrate the great variety which will characterise mankind in resurrection? Whereas every saint will be raised with certain inalienable characteristics (vv.42-44), there will nevertheless be a great diversity in function and sphere of glory. Some will be blessed in the heavenly places, others in the New Jerusalem or on the new earth, each according to his calling and reward. Each will be given the body of God's choosing and each will be satisfied with the place assigned to him. The glory of one may differ from another, but no one will complain that he is deficient in glory!

15:42b-49: *So it is with the resurrection of the dead. What is sown is perishable; what is raised is imperishable. It is sown in dishonour; it is raised in glory. It is sown in weakness; it is raised in power. It is sown a natural body; it is raised a spiritual body. If there is a natural body, there is also a spiritual body. Thus it is written, "The first man Adam became a living being"; the last*

Adam became a life-giving spirit. But it is not the spiritual that is first but the natural, and then the spiritual. The first man was from the earth, a man of dust; the second man is from heaven. As was the man of dust, so also are those who are of the dust, and as is the man of heaven, so also are those who are of heaven. Just as we have born the image of the man of dust, we shall also bear the image of the man of heaven.

We already know what the resurrection body will be like from the Lord's resurrection body as described in the Gospels, for we shall bear the same image, the image of the Man of (and from) heaven (see also Philippians 3:20-21). In some respects our bodies will be the same as they are now. If our faces are not immediately recognizable, it will only be because all the lines of sorrow, wear and age will have gone.

So it was in the case of Jesus though there may have been other reasons why the two from Emmaus failed to recognize Him (Luke 24:16). But it won't be long before we are recognized by our friends and relations, and we too will recognize them. There are four big differences which are mentioned in these verses between our present body and the one we shall receive.

(1)   It is sown perishable, raised imperishable. Our present bodies are perishable, corruptible, but as the apostle says in verse 50, the perishable cannot inherit the imperishable kingdom of God. Our present bodies, buried in the earth, will disintegrate and perish, but they will be raised imperishable, fit for God's presence and kingdom. In resurrection we shall be eternally youthful, for ever growing wiser, but never any older!

(2)   It is sown in dishonour, raised in glory. Growing ever older and feebler, possibly senile, finally dying and being buried out of sight if not out of mind, what could be more degrading than that? But all that pain and shame will be forgotten on that resurrection morning. The sufferings of this

present time are not worthy to be compared with the glory to be revealed in us. Then the creation itself will be set free from its bondage to decay and will share the freedom and glory of the children of God (Romans 8:18-25).

(3)   It is sown in weakness, raised in power. The stupendous power which God exercised in raising Christ from the dead will then be exercised in those who believe (Ephesians 1:19-20). We shall then know His resurrection power (Phil. 3:10) to an extent inconceivable in this life.

(4)   It is sown a natural body, raised a spiritual body. Our Lord's resurrection body was spiritual, but not in the sense of non-material. He could eat fish and be touched, but at the same time He could pass through closed doors, appearing and disappearing at will. Our spiritual

bodies will be like His, suffused and sustained by the Spirit, overflowing with the life of the Spirit. As we know from Genesis 2:7 the first man Adam became a living soul when God breathed into his nostrils the breath of life. The last man, Christ, became in resurrection a life-making Spirit, and that is why in Christ all men will be *made alive* in the first or second resurrections (15:22). "For as the Father raises the dead and *makes them alive*, so also the Son *makes alive* whom he will" (John 5:21).

We shall then bear the image of the Man of heaven (49). Even now we are being transformed into the same image from one degree of glory to another (2 Cor. 3:18), being (continuously) renewed in knowledge after the image of our Creator (Col. 3:10). In resurrection the process will be completed. The image of the first Adam, the man of dust, will have passed away and been replaced by the image of the Man from heaven.

15:50-55: *I tell you this, brothers: flesh and blood cannot inherit the kingdom of God, nor does the perishable inherit the imperishable. Behold! I tell you a mystery. We shall not all sleep, but we shall all be changed, in a moment, in the twinkling of an eye, at the last trumpet. For the trumpet will sound, and the dead will be raised imperishable, and we shall be changed. For this perishable body must put on the imperishable, and this mortal body must put on immortality. When the perishable puts on the imperishable, and the mortal puts on immortality, then shall come to pass the saying that is written: "Death is swallowed up in victory." "O death, where is your victory? O death, where is your sting?"*

Flesh and blood cannot inherit the kingdom of God. In resurrection we shall be different in many respects. The flesh will be of a more refined texture and the blood will be replaced by the life-giving Holy Spirit. Our Lord could pass through closed doors (John 20:19), yet Thomas was able to feel the nail holes and put his hand in the Lord's side (20:27). In order to inherit the kingdom of

God our present bodies of flesh and blood will have to be changed or exchanged as the case may be. In the case of those who have died, the old body will be exchanged for a new body in resurrection, but in the case of those who are still alive, a remarkable transformation will take place as the apostle goes on to explain.

"We shall not all sleep", he says, "but we shall be changed, in a moment, in the twinkling of an eye, at the last trumpet."

The apostle speaks of those who are still alive at the second coming of Christ, and he clearly includes himself. At that time the second coming was expected in the not too distant future, certainly before the demise of that generation as Jesus Himself had indicated (Matt. 24:34). But, as we know, there was a change of purpose on God's part when the Jewish people made it abundantly clear that they wanted no part in their Messiah or the salvation which He had come to bring them: holding out His hands all day long to a disobedient and contrary people (Romans 10:21).

This came to a head, we believe, at the end of Acts, and it was not long after that the truth of the Body was revealed to Paul in his Roman prison. The hope of the Lord's return was then postponed for an indefinite period, but hopefully one day soon it will take place as promised, and the "mystery" programme of change and "putting on", described here, will be fulfilled to the letter.

When the last trumpet sounds two events will take place:

- the dead will be raised imperishable and
- the living will be changed.

This subject is dealt with more fully in 1 Thessalonians 4:13-18. Paul there reveals the word of the Lord on this important matter. The dead in Christ will rise first, then "we who are alive" will be caught up into the clouds, there to meet the Lord in the air.

The nature of the change which will take place is described as a "putting on". This perishable body must put on the imperishable, and this mortal body must put on immortality. This is what will happen to those who are still alive. They will be clothed with their resurrection bodies without, so to speak, taking off their present mortal bodies. This is precisely how the apostle describes it in 2 Corinthians 5:1-5. He says there,

> "For while we are still in this tent, we groan, being burdened – not that we would be unclothed [in death], but that we would be further clothed, so that what is mortal may be swallowed up by life."

Death is here described as an unclothing, taking off the clothes (*ekdusasthai*), but the transformation as an over-clothing, putting on an additional garment over the present one (*ependusasthai*). This is what Peter did when he put on his outer garment (*ton ependuten*) before throwing himself into the sea (John 21:7). It is only an analogy of course.

A snake does the opposite: it takes off its outer garment to reveal the new snake underneath. Paul could have used that analogy, but shedding one's skin is more suggestive of dying. Both death and resurrection are pictured in the snake's shuffling off its mortal coil to reveal the new man underneath.

In this way "what is mortal" (*to thneton*, as in 1 Cor. 15:53 and 54) will be swallowed up by life. Then will come to pass what is written,

"Death is *swallowed up* in victory" (15:54).

Enoch and Elijah had a foretaste of this when they were taken up to heaven, but even they have not yet put on the imperishable and immortality as described here. This they will receive at the last trump when the living saints are caught up into the clouds to meet the Lord in the air.

A similar change transformed our Lord's body. He had in fact died, but His body had not seen corruption as both Peter and Paul saw fit to emphasise (Acts 2:31; 13:37). It was the same body that rose from the dead, though wonderfully changed and glorified. His resurrection is the prototype both of those who die and of those who remain alive. For all those who have died He is the pattern and exemplar of resurrection, but for those who remain alive He is the pattern and exemplar of transformation.

Exultantly the apostle quotes Isaiah 25:8 and Hosea 13:14:

> "Death is swallowed up in victory. O death, where is your victory? O death, where is your sting?"

With the "first resurrection" the impotence of death will be demonstrated as all the believing dead are raised to new life in Christ. But death itself, the final enemy, is not destroyed for another thousand years (15:26). Christ will reign until He has subdued all His enemies of whatever kind, the last of these being death itself.

15:56-57: *The sting of death is sin, and the power of sin is the law. But thanks be to God, who gives us the victory through our Lord Jesus Christ.*

Even now God is giving us the victory through our

Lord Jesus Christ. The sting of death is sin and the power of sin is the Law. Sin came into the world through one man and death through sin, and so death spread to all men because all men sinned (Romans 5:12). It is sin that brought death into the world and sin that keeps it there. And the Law only made matters worse by spelling out what constituted sin. Paul admits that apart from the law he would not have known sin.

> "Sin, seizing an opportunity through the commandment, deceived me and through it killed me" (Romans 7:11).

It is a vicious circle: the Law which promised life only served to promote sinfulness, and sin in turn produces death. Christ, however, has squared the circle by dying for sin and rising from the dead. Instead of being serial sinners, we are now more than conquerors through Him who loved us! (Romans 8:37)

15:58: *Therefore, my beloved brothers, be steadfast, immovable, always abounding in the work of the Lord, knowing that in the Lord your*

If there is no resurrection of the dead ... What then? 61

labour is not in vain.

At the beginning of this chapter the apostle reminded them of the gospel which they had believed and embraced and by which they were saved – *provided that* they held it fast. Now, in conclusion, he urges them to remain steadfast and immovable, especially in their belief and teaching on resurrection, and also to be always abounding in the work of the Lord. Everyone who obeys these instructions will know for sure that his labour in the Lord is not in vain.

A similar exhortation is placed before the Colossian church. It is, he says, God's desire

> "to present you holy and blameless and above reproach before him, *if indeed* you continue in the faith, stable and *steadfast*, *not shifting* from the hope of the gospel that you heard" (Col. 1:22-23).

In both places he speaks of the hope of the gospel and he stresses the importance of remaining steadfast and unmoveable.

We may fittingly close with the words of Romans 15:13,

> "May the God of hope fill you with all joy and peace in believing, so that by the power of the Holy Spirit you may abound in hope."

If there is no resurrection of the dead ... What then? 64

Conclusion

Conclusion

Paul addresses his Corinthian detractors as "foolish" (v.36). Their folly was that of holding on to out-worn ideas which they had accepted from childhood and were unwilling to relinquish.

However, today, I see the tenacious hold of preconceived ideas on those who call themselves Christians. Many refuse to take seriously any idea which runs contrary to what they currently believe. You of course, diligent reader, are free from this impediment (or so you may think!), but in fact none of us are free.

We all need to keep an open mind, not only to receive new ideas but also to give up old ideas if need be, ideas which do not conform to what *the Bible* teaches. Let us therefore discern by testing what is the good and acceptable and perfect will of God, and so be transformed by the renewing of our minds (Romans 12:2).

We do not know how many of the Corinthian believers were prepared to accept Paul's teaching on resurrection, but there is no reason why any of us should be unwilling to do so.

More on
1 Corinthians 15

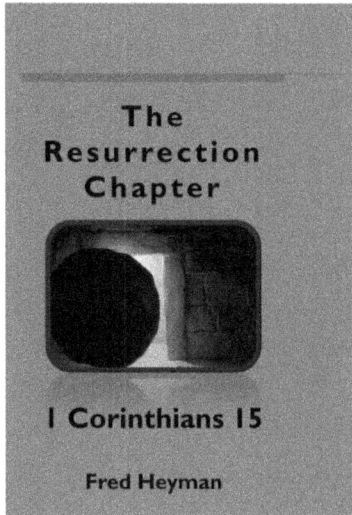

The Resurrection Chapter

1 Corinthians 15

By Fred Heyman

In this book the author reminds us that Paul's teaching on the resurrection of Christ is based upon

(a) the Old Testament,

(b) the revelation he had had of the risen Christ, and

(c) eyewitness account of others.

If there is no resurrection of the dead ... What then? 69

He also shows that the future resurrection of believers is based upon the past resurrection of Christ, Who is the firstfruits of those who are to rise from the dead. This resurrection is assured by belief in the gospel of salvation, which is clearly expressed in the opening verses of 1 Corinthians 15, and it takes place when Christ returns, a recurring theme later in the chapter.

Further details of this book, and the ones on the next pages, can be seen on

www.obt.org.uk

They can be ordered from that website and also from

The Open Bible Trust,
Fordland Mount, Upper Basildon,
Reading, RG8 8LU, UK.

They are also available as eBooks
from Amazon and Apple
and as KDP paperbacks from Amazon.

More on Resurrection

Resurrection! When?
Michael and Sylvia Penny

Immortality! When?
Michael Penny

When was Christ's death and resurrection?
Peter John-Charles

The Path to Immortality
Rowland Wickes

About the Author

Charles Ozanne was born in Crowborough, Sussex, in 1936. He read Theology at Oxford before undertaking research in the book of Revelation for his PhD at the University of Manchester under F. F. Bruce. Some of his recent publications for the Open Bible Trust have been a commentary on Daniel, entitled *Empires of the End-Time;* a critique of Replacement Theology entitled *God's Plan for Israel: Replacement or Restoration?* And a work looking at *The Sabbath and Circumcision.* A major work, *The Believer's Guide to Bible Chronology* has been published by *Authorhouse. H*owever, it is available from the Open Bible Trust.

His latest work is *Understanding the New Testament.* A well-written and well-presented commentary on the whole of the New Testament, showing that each of the 27 documents, although distinctive, fit into an overall pattern. For further details of this latest book, and others, please visit:

www.obt.org.uk

Charles Ozanne is a regular contributor to
Search magazine

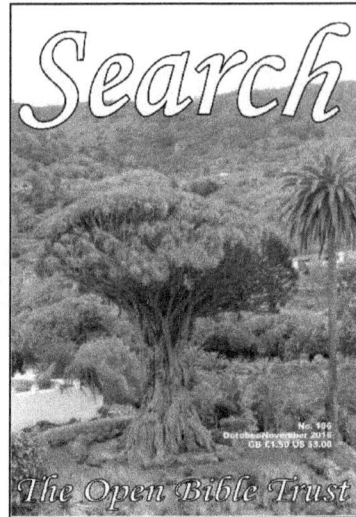

For a free sample of
The Open Bible Trust's magazine *Search,*
please email

admin@obt.org.uk

or visit

www.obt.org.uk

Also by Charles Ozanne

The following is a selection.

Israel's Appointed Feasts

Sensational Truth in Ephesians

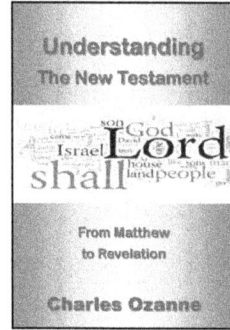

Understanding The New Testament
From Matthew to Revelation

****

For more information on these please visit
www.obt.org.uk

They can be ordered from that website and from
The Open Bible Trust
Fordland Mount, Upper Basildon,
Reading, RG8 8LU, UK.

If there is no resurrection of the dead ... What then? 75

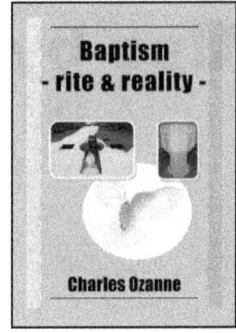

God's Plan for Israel:
Replacement or Restoration?

Empires of the End-Times
Through Daniel's Telescopic Lens

Baptism:
Rite and reality

****

**These books are also available as
eBooks from Amazon and Apple**

And as KDP paperback from Amazon

About this Book

If there is no resurrection of the dead ...
What then?
(An exposition of 1 Corinthians 15)

What is the most distinctive, attractive, and far-reaching doctrine that Christians believe? For the author the answer is **the resurrection.**

Though not exclusively Christian, since both Judaism and Islam have a doctrine of resurrection of their own, it is nevertheless the most *distinctive* of all Christian beliefs, and certainly the founder of no other religion claims to have risen from the dead.

It is the most *attractive* because it holds out the promise of eternal life on the other side of the grave. And it is the most *far-reaching* because the resurrection life goes on for ever and ever!

If there is no resurrection of the dead ... What then? 77

That is why 1 Corinthians 15 is such an important chapter. This chapter tackles the whole subject of resurrection against the backdrop of some who denied or doubted there was any such thing. To the Greek way of thinking bodily resurrection was a ludicrous idea, and there were Jews also, the Sadducees in particular (Acts 23:8), who entertained the same scepticism.

If there is no resurrection of the dead ... What then?   79

Publications of The Open Bible Trust must be in accordance with its evangelical, fundamental and dispensational basis. However, beyond this minimum, writers are free to express whatever beliefs they may have as their own understanding, provided that the aim in so doing is to further the object of The Open Bible Trust. A copy of the doctrinal basis is available on **www.obt.org.uk** or from:

THE OPEN BIBLE TRUST
Fordland Mount, Upper Basildon,
Reading, RG8 8LU, GB

www.ingramcontent.com/pod-product-compliance
Lightning Source LLC
Chambersburg PA
CBHW060652030426
42337CB00017B/2572